GREATEST FOOTBALL STARS

Published in the UK by Sweet Cherry Publishing Limited, 2024
Unit 36, Vulcan House, Vulcan Road,
Leicester LE5 3EF, United Kingdom

Unit 31, The Pottery, Bakers Point,
Pottery Road, Dún Laoghaire,
Dublin A96 EV18, Ireland

2 4 6 8 10 9 7 5 3 1

ISBN: 978-1-80263-537-9

Greatest Football Stars:
Lionel Messi

Text by Luke Paton
Illustrations by Sophie Jones

www.sweetcherrypublishing.com

Printed and bound in India

Sweet
Cherry

LIONEL
MESSI

THE UNOFFICIAL STORY

WRITTEN BY
LUKE PATON

CONTENTS

A DIFFICULT DIAGNOSIS

Lionel Messi was crying.

Dr Schwarzstein had just told the eleven-year-old boy that he suffered from growth hormone deficiency. Lionel didn't understand.

He tried to listen as the doctor explained. He supposed it had

something to do with him being small for his age. His football teammates always teased him because he was shorter than every other kid on the pitch!

But now Dr Schwarzstein was saying he might not grow much taller than he already was. It was a disaster! His football coaches already worried that he wouldn't be strong enough to play against bigger boys. This diagnosis could mean his career was over before it had even begun!

Then Dr Schwarzstein smiled.

Lionel's chest filled with hope.

Dr Schwarzstein said he had a plan. All Lionel had to do was inject himself with a growth hormone twice a day.

'Will I grow?' Lionel asked, wiping away his tears.

'You will be taller than Maradona,' Dr Schwarzstein replied.

That was all Lionel needed to hear. He thought Diego Maradona was the best football player in the world, and Maradona was only 1.65 metres tall!

'I don't know if you are going to be *better* than Maradona,' the doctor added with a wink, 'but you'll be taller than him.'

He handed Lionel a small white box with a syringe inside. 'Here it is,' he said.

Lionel took the box home and started his injections right away. The needle on the syringe was only small, and Lionel didn't think the injections hurt too much. No worse than getting a little mosquito bite! Besides, if it meant he could carry on playing football, Lionel would do anything.

Lionel had been playing football almost since he could walk!

LET HIM PLAY!

Lionel Andrés Messi was born on the 24th of June 1987 in Rosario, Argentina, to Celia Cuccittini and Jorge Messi.

He had two older brothers, Rodrigo and Matias, and a younger sister, Maria Sol. There were no

professional footballers in the Messi family. His mother worked in manufacturing, and his father in a steel factory. But the family loved football – like everybody in Argentina – and all the Messi boys joined the local football club, Abanderado Grandoli.

Lionel was only four years old when he played his first match for them. He was a lot smaller than the other boys, and the coaches didn't want him to play.

'He's too small,' they said.

Luckily, Lionel's grandmother wouldn't take no for an answer. 'Let him play,' she argued. 'Let him play!'

She noticed that one of the teams was missing a player, so she kept hassling the coaches to use Lionel.

Finally, they let Lionel onto the pitch ... and he didn't let his grandmother down.

He scored two goals!

The coaches didn't leave Lionel out again. Even though he was a small boy, Lionel's talent was too big for him to stay on the sidelines. He loved scoring goals, and the coaches loved him for his talent!

When Lionel turned six years old, he moved to his first major club: Newell's Old Boys – or 'Nuls', as local people call them. The team is a big deal in Argentina, and one of the largest clubs in the area. They recognised Lionel's ability and wanted him on their side.

At Newell's Old Boys, Lionel started playing in a team with other boys his age. He was the smallest, of course, but that didn't stop him from making friends in the squad.

One of his closest friends was Lucas Scaglia. They'd play football at Newell's, then hang out at his house. Lionel especially liked going to Lucas's house when his cousin was there.

Her name was Antonela Roccuzzo.

Lionel called her Anto, and the other boys teased him about how much he liked her. He'd go red and say nothing. He was already shy, and he didn't want to talk about girls!

Lionel told his friends he just wanted to focus on football. Fortunately for him, Newell's Old Boys played some of the best football in Rosario! Lionel was the star, but the rest of the team were so amazing that fans gave them a special name: La Maquina del '87, which translates to 'The Machine of '87'.

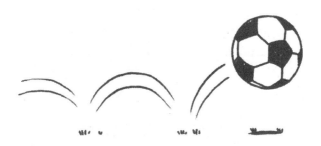

THE MACHINE OF '87

There was no other club Lionel wanted to play for more than Newell's Old Boys. He even got a Newell's Old Boys shirt for his very first birthday!

His debut with the youth side was one of the best ever. Lionel scored four times, and Newell's Old Boys won

the game 6-0! Newell's played 'baby football', or seven-a-side matches, and nobody could get close to Lionel when he played! The Machine of '87 didn't lose a game of 'baby football' for three years.

Even when they started playing eleven-a-side matches, the team was feared all over South America. Crowds of fans would gather to watch Lionel bamboozle the opposition, and to watch the Machine of '87 notch up another victory.

In those three years, Newell's won all the local competitions, and in one season they went twenty points clear at the top of their league. They'd travel to other countries to play in tournaments, and they'd beat their opponents there, too. They were unstoppable!

Lionel scored in most of the games he played. He'd get angry when he couldn't score or when his teammates didn't pass him the ball. On the rare occasion Newell's lost, Lionel would burst into tears. Football was his life, and so was winning!

People from all over started to hear about how good he was.

One boy in Rosario got especially tired of everybody talking about Lionel. 'Who is this Messi?' the boy complained. 'You talk so much about him. Bring him here!'

When Lionel and the boy finally played against each other, Lionel embarrassed the boy by nutmegging him twice!

The biggest game Newell's Old Boys played every season was against the nearby Rosario Central. Any competitive meeting between the two clubs is called a Clásico Rosarino, and their rivalry is legendary in Argentina. Even the youth teams despise each other!

Lionel's reputation was getting so big at Newell's that he'd really suffer during these matches. Argentinian football can be rough and physical at the best of times. But when you're playing in a match like the Clásico Rosarino, you're lucky to come home without any fresh lumps and bumps!

In one game, Lionel performed five 'sombreros' on the same defender, which is when you flick the ball over another player's head. The defender's father was furious!

But Lionel survived that game, and many others like it. In the 176 games he played for the his club's youth team, Lionel scored 234 goals. That's an average of 1.33 goals every single game. He was becoming such a phenomenon that the Newell's Old Boys first team had him entertain the crowd before their matches. He'd do keepy-uppies on the centre spot for up to fifteen minutes while fans cheered

and tossed him coins.

But off the pitch, Lionel was haunted by the problem of his size. He was still not as tall as the other players and his coaches were very worried.

The team put a call in to Dr Schwarzstein. 'We're sending you the best player that we have,' they said. They wanted to know whether there was anything that could be done about Lionel's small stature. That's

when the doctor ran tests on Lionel and discovered the young boy had growth hormone deficiency.

Lionel's parents showed Lionel how to do the injections for the first few times. One night they'd inject one of his legs. The next night they'd inject the other. Eventually, Lionel learnt how to do the injections himself.

But Lionel's father spotted another problem Lionel hadn't thought of: the injections were expensive. The Messi family were barely getting by as it was and they couldn't afford the injections on their own.

What were they going to do? Lionel wouldn't be able to play football if he didn't get the treatment ... but the family couldn't afford to eat if they paid for the injections!

Newell's Old Boys stepped in at first. They needed Lionel as part of the Machine of '87, so they took care of Lionel's medical bills ... for a time. Argentina fell into a financial crisis and money started to get tight for everybody. After a while, Newell's Old Boys said they could no longer afford Lionel's treatments.

Jorge, Lionel's father, was devastated. *I have to do something,* he thought.

Then one day in September 2000, Lionel didn't turn up for training with Newell's.

Nobody on the team knew where he was or what he was doing.

It was a mystery.

As far as anybody knew, Lionel Messi had gone missing.

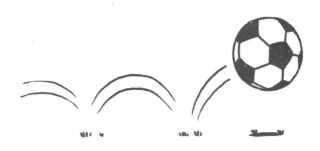

4
CAMP NOU CALLING

'What's up with Messi?'

It was the question every player at Newell's Old Boys was asking. Lionel hadn't turned up for training for ages. He never normally missed training, and now he hadn't been around in close to a month!

A concerned father called up the Messi household. 'What's up with Leo?' he asked. 'He is not coming to practice.'

'He can't go to practice,' Lionel's mother, Celia, replied. 'He's sick.'

After another week of missed training, the father tried asking Celia again. 'Where's Leo?'

'He's still sick,' said his mother.

Many rumours flew around the Newell's Old Boys camp about Lionel's mysterious illness, but none of them were true. In fact, Lionel wasn't sick at all.

He was trying out for FC Barcelona. The famous Spanish club had seen tapes of Lionel playing football, and they liked what they saw. The coaches invited him to do a trial for Barcelona in September 2000 so they could get a closer look at him.

Jorge knew a club as big as Barcelona could take his son to new heights in football. He also knew they could afford to pay for Lionel's

hormone treatment. It was a win-win situation, and he didn't doubt Lionel would breeze through the trial!

It took Jorge and Lionel twenty-four hours to get from Rosario, Argentina, to Barcelona, Spain. And as soon as their plane landed, Lionel had to trek to Barcelona's training ground.

As usual, Lionel was much smaller than the other players trying out for Barcelona. The group included future stars Gerard Piqué and Cesc Fàbregas.

We're going to eat him alive! they thought after seeing how small he was.

But the moment Lionel touched the

ball, the others realised they were in the presence of genius. It was almost as if the ball was glued to Lionel's feet!

'It's impossible to get the ball off him!' said one teammate.

The most important person Lionel had to impress was Carles Rexach, the technical director for Barcelona's first team. And fortunately, Rexach knew a star when he saw one. 'You can sign him up,' he told the club. 'He is fuera de serie – outstanding.'

Barcelona not only agreed to sign Lionel and set up his family in an apartment in Spain, but they also covered Lionel's medical treatments. It was a dream come true!

His new life in Spain was about to begin.

5

FINDING HIS FEET

Lionel's parents and siblings would be moving to Spain with him, so it was a very exciting opportunity for them all.

On the day the Messi family left Rosario, everybody in the neighbourhood came out to say

goodbye to them. Lionel cried and cried. Even though he was going to Spain to fulfill his dream, the pain of leaving behind everything he knew was too much.

Before leaving Rosario, Lionel made sure that he said goodbye to Dr Schwarzstein.

Lionel gave the doctor a signed number 9 Newell's Old Boys shirt. It was the number Lionel had worn when he played for the club, and he thought it might be worth something when he made it big in Barcelona.

'Good luck,' the doctor said.

Lionel cried the rest of the way to the airport and even on the plane. Was this all going to be worth it? Did he want to see this crazy football dream through? Would he see Lucas's cousin, Antonela, ever again? He didn't know, but it felt like the end of something big.

Jorge was worried about his son. 'Do you want to go home?' he asked.

Lionel thought about it … and shook his head. 'I want to see it through,' he replied.

The first few days of training with the Barcelona youth side were very hard. He felt like the other boys didn't want him there. They already had their own friends because they all lived and trained together at La Masia, the club's training facilities.

'I can't understand them!' Lionel complained. 'They all speak Catalan!'

He even thought some of the coaches didn't want him there. He heard that one coach had told the other players to be tough with Lionel in his first training sessions. The coach didn't like the way Lionel played. 'One touch!' he would yell at Lionel. 'Don't dribble so much!'

Lionel didn't listen to him. He played the way that came naturally to him, and that meant dribbling a lot! He just kept his head down, his mouth shut and let his football do his talking.

He could tell it annoyed the other defenders, though. They'd thunder towards him, desperate to foul him, and Lionel would skilfully shift the ball and slip away. He was too quick for them! The defenders would be left standing in his dust.

Those skills impressed the coaches, but they didn't exactly help Lionel fit in with the other players. One time, the other boys hid his PlayStation from him and wouldn't give it back. Lionel was so upset that he started to cry! He felt like he was never going to fit in with this new team.

 As soon as he went back to his apartment after training, he'd lock himself in his bedroom and sob.

He didn't want his father to hear him cry because he was afraid of letting him down.

He didn't want his teammates to see him cry because he was afraid they'd make fun of him.

Everything was so hard! He missed his family and friends back home.

The rest of his family were struggling to settle into their new home, too. Matias wanted to go back to Argentina to be with his girlfriend. Maria Sol was getting picked on at school because she couldn't understand Catalan. The family

were so unhappy that Celia, Rodrigo, Matias and Maria Sol decided to return to Argentina.

Jorge and Lionel stayed in Spain while Lionel continued his training with Barcelona. Lionel loved having his father by his side, but it would be better to also have some friends his own age!

Then, just when Lionel thought it couldn't get any worse, things started to change.

Lionel clicked with the most talented players on the pitch. In the 2002/2003 season, Lionel played in the Cadete A league for the Barcelona under 16s side. Two of the other stars of this team were Fàbregas and Piqué. The trio were so deadly even as fifteen-year-olds that people called the side the 'Baby Dream Team'.

The Baby Dream Team was invincible that season. Lionel played in thirty-seven matches and scored an incredible thirty goals. He

helped the team win the Spanish and Catalan Championships as well as the league.

No other team had ever done that before!

Lionel was still smaller than most of his teammates, but he didn't worry about his height anymore. The Barcelona club doctor said he could stop taking the injections and just monitor his diet and keep fit. Dr Schwarzstein had been right: Lionel grew to 1.70 metres – a whole five centimetres taller than Maradona!

He was still lonely, and he still cried after talking to his mother on the telephone. But he was going places, and the team finally accepted him as one of their own. His teammates called him enano, which means 'small one', and they meant it nicely!

In November 2003, Lionel got called over by the Barcelona Academy team co-ordinator, Josep Colomer. Lionel thought Colomer was going to give him the usual coaching tips.

He had no idea that his life was about to change forever.

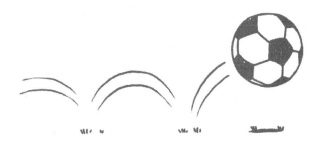

6

A DREAM
DEBUT

'You'll be travelling with the first
team,' Colomer said.

He explained that the Barcelona
first team was playing a friendly
against Porto. The manager, Frank
Rijkaard, wanted some of the
younger boys from the youth teams

to play in the match, and Lionel was going to be one of those lucky players!

'You should enjoy everything,' Colomer said. 'There's no reason to make any changes – just continue in the same way. Enjoy the game and the experience.'

It was everything Lionel had ever wanted. Finally, a chance to play in the first team!

But Colomer did have a warning for the young star: 'When you come back, you should concentrate on the youth team again.'

Lionel nodded and said thank you. He stayed calm on the outside, but inside he was bursting with excitement.

The night before the match, he could barely sleep he was so nervous. He knew he was going to be a substitute and that there was no guarantee he'd play. But still, this was Barcelona's first team!

As the game started, Lionel watched from the bench, his hands held together to stop them from shaking. As the minutes ticked

over, he started to think that maybe
he wouldn't get a chance to play,
after all.

Then, towards the end of the
match, the manager told him to
come on. Lionel leapt to his feet.
He suddenly felt ridiculous in a
Barcelona shirt that was way too big
for him and hair that wouldn't stop
flopping around. But that wasn't
going to stop him from trying his
absolute best!

Lionel's time on the pitch went by in
a blur. He didn't get on the scoresheet,
but he did manage to get a shot in.

He played well, and he knew the coaches and the fans had noticed him.

'He reminds one of Maradona,' a commentator said. This wouldn't be the last time someone would make that comparison!

Lionel didn't have to wait long to make his competitive debut for Barcelona. On the 16th of October 2004, Lionel was again on the subs bench while Barcelona played

Espanyol in a Catalan derby match. Barcelona was winning 1-0 when, in the 82nd minute, Lionel

got the sign from the manager that he was going to play.

The crowd had no idea who he was.

'What's his name?' they asked.

'Never heard of him ...'

'Someone from the B team.'

'What on earth ...? A child!'

It was true: Lionel was still only seventeen. He was the youngest player to ever play for Barcelona!

The fans weren't convinced.

After he came on, he got the ball and two players from Espanyol approached him. Most players would have thought they had nowhere to go, but Lionel wasn't most players. With the ball seemingly attached to his feet, he dribbled his way out of the situation and left the two players tackling thin air.

The doubters in the crowd were silenced. Lionel played ten minutes of competitive football and marked himself as one to watch.

'That's for my mother, who's back in Argentina,' Lionel said

after the match. 'I will remember those ten minutes my whole life.'

Lionel made his starting debut for Barcelona the following year. It was a Joan Gamper Trophy match against Juventus, and the Italian side was full of stars such as Patrick Vieira, Giorgio Chiellini and Fabio Cannavaro.

But after the match, people were only talking about Lionel.

During the game, Lionel ran rings around Vieira and tormented Chiellini. The only way the Juventus team could stop him was by fouling him.

'Messi! Messi! Messi!' the Barcelona fans in their Camp Nou stadium chanted.

'Where did that little devil come from?' asked the Juventus manager, Fabio Capello.

At the end of the game, Capello approached the Barcelona manager, Rijkaard. 'Can we loan Lionel for the season?' he asked.

'No chance,' said Rijkaard.

The team knew he was going to be a star, too. When Lionel first appeared in the team's changing room, he'd sit alone in the corner, not wanting to join in with the other players. Barcelona had legendary players such as Portuguese midfielder Deco and

Brazilian striker Ronaldinho. It was a scary changing room for someone so young and shy!

But one day, Ronaldinho broke the ice. He called to him, 'Leo! Leo!' He made a space for Lionel in the changing room and forced him to sit with the rest of the squad. It was the start of an amazing friendship Lionel would treasure forever.

Sometimes Ronaldinho would even comb Lionel's floppy hair.

'Why don't you comb my hair?' another player joked.

'Because you're not going to be famous, but he is,' Ronaldinho teased. 'You'll never be the best player in the world, but he will.'

He was always joking around to make Lionel and the rest of the team feel relaxed. But he also knew how good Lionel could be.

'Play with happiness,' Ronaldinho would tell Lionel. 'Play free. Just play with the ball.'

Ronaldinho also knew something else.

On the 1st of May 2005, he told Lionel, 'You'll score today.'

Barcelona was playing Albacete, and Lionel came on as a substitute in the 87th minute. He had a goal disallowed in the 89th minute. Then in the 91st minute, he got on the end of a chip pass from Ronaldinho and found the back of the net.

It was an incredible moment. He was the youngest goalscorer in Barcelona's history!

Lionel jumped on Ronaldinho's back and pumped his arms with joy. The rest of the team ran around to

rub his head and pound his back!
It was glorious!

'You'll never forget your first goal,'
Ronaldinho said. 'And you'll have to
remember me because I passed you
the ball!'

GOING FOR GOLD

When Lionel joined the Argentina U20s team, future Manchester City superstar Sergio Agüero was part of the squad. Agüero played football in Argentina and didn't follow the Spanish teams, so he'd never heard of Lionel.

'What was your name?' Agüero asked him.

'Lionel,' he said.

'What a ridiculous name!' Agüero laughed. 'What about your last name?'

'Messi,' he answered.

The rest of the team was shocked. Everybody had been talking about the boy genius from Barcelona.

'This is him?' Agüero said, doubtfully.

Before the end of the next training session, Agüero knew exactly who Lionel was!

Lionel's first major international

tournament was the 2005 FIFA World Youth Championship in the Netherlands. Coach Francisco Ferraro started Lionel on the bench for their first match against the United States … and the United States won the game 1-0.

The only good part of the match was that Lionel played very well in the second half. Ferraro put him in the

starting lineup after that … and Argentina won every game! Lionel scored six goals in the

tournament, including two penalty kicks in the final. That meant he was the highest scorer in the competition!

Agüero couldn't believe how calm Lionel looked when he took those high-pressure penalties in the final.

'That was incredible!' he said. 'You hit them as if you were in your back garden!'

Lionel celebrated the second penalty by dedicating it to his sister, his cousin and his young nephews. He lifted his Argentina shirt to reveal a white undershirt with their names on it.

Lionel thought this was the best moment of his career so far ...

But the fans could tell he was only just getting started!

'How did he manage that?' supporters at Barcelona's Camp Nou would ask week in and week out.

'What will Messi do this time?' they wondered.

The newspapers even started asking him whether he thought he was the best player in the world.

'I still have a lot of room for improvement,' Lionel would tell them, modestly. 'I want to shoot equally well with both feet. I could also do with learning how to take free kicks like Ronaldinho.'

But Barcelona fans already thought Lionel was the new Ronaldinho. Even though he was still only twenty-one, Lionel was the team's star player. The supporters wanted to see him start every single game!

Lionel wanted that as well, but before Barcelona was due to start the 2008/2009 season, Lionel had the chance to play in the

Olympics for Argentina. He really wanted to go … if his club would let him!

Barcelona was worried because the Olympics clashed with their Champions League matches. If Lionel went to the Olympics, he wouldn't be available to help them win the most important trophy in European football.

But Barcelona manager Pep Guardiola knew what it meant to Lionel to represent his country. After all, Guardiola had won an Olympic gold medal for Spain in 1992. He spoke to Lionel after Barcelona's pre-season friendly against Fiorentina.

'You want to go to the Olympics, don't you?' he asked.

'Yes,' said Lionel.

And that was that.

Lionel joined the Argentinian team to prepare for the world-renowned competition. The chance to win a gold medal – he couldn't wait!

Lionel was blown away by how different the Olympics was to regular football. The Argentina team stayed in the Olympic Village where all the other athletes from all the other sports stayed. One day, he saw the iconic American basketball player Kobe Bryant.

'Hola! Soy Kobe,' Kobe said, speaking Spanish.

Lionel talked to him for a while, then, just before Kobe left, he called back, 'Messi, you're the best!'

And Lionel proved he was among the best in the world during the Olympics. He scored the first goal for Argentina in that competition and assisted a couple more. In the quarter-final match against the Netherlands, he fired in one of his greatest goals.

He left two opposition defenders behind, slipped past another, then scored from an impossible angle. It felt so good!

But the semi-final was bittersweet.

It was sweet because he helped the team beat Brazil 3-0. But it was bitter because Ronaldinho, his friend and idol, was playing for Brazil. After the final whistle blew, he hugged Ronaldinho and wished him all the best.

'It feels really good to be in the final,' Lionel said. 'I didn't imagine we could score like this. Now we are ready for gold.'

They were more than ready. Lionel had a great game in the final against Nigeria – and even provided the assist for the winning goal.

Argentina won the gold!

Lionel couldn't stop smiling as the gold medal was hung around his neck after the game. He sang, danced and chanted along with the rest of the team. It was party time, and the celebrations lasted long into the night!

8

THE GREATEST OF ALL TIME

Before Guardiola even met Lionel, a senior player told him, 'There's a an exceptional player in the squad. He's very young, but he scores many goals.'

The new Barcelona manager wasn't so sure. He'd first seen Lionel in a shop with his father and thought he was short and shy.

Is this one as good as they say? he wondered.

But when Lionel played in some pre-season matches, Guardiola knew he had a star in his team. *With him, we will win everything,* he thought.

But Pep worried that Barcelona had lost their discipline. The team was no longer playing their best football.

Ronaldinho and Deco were masters of the game, but they weren't the

most professional players when it came to training.

It wasn't a surprise to Guardiola that they weren't playing as well as they used to, because he felt they weren't trying as hard as they used to.

But Pep's biggest worry was that his star player, Lionel, was friends with Ronaldinho and Deco. He thought Lionel might fall under their spell and lose his form as well.

The situation has gotten worse, and the solution is to build a strong changing room, thought Pep.

He let Ronaldinho transfer to AC Milan and Deco transfer to Chelsea. Then he focussed on Lionel. For one thing, he knew Lionel's diet wasn't helping his fitness.

Lionel loved going to a restaurant in Barcelona that served great Argentinian steak. He couldn't remember how many years he'd been eating at the restaurant, but he'd go there almost every night. His order was always the same: steak and cola!

Guardiola put an end to that after he took charge of Barcelona. He told the steak restaurant not to serve Lionel anymore, and he told Lionel he had to start eating properly.

The new manager didn't just single out Lionel, though. He fined any member of the squad who was late to training or didn't follow his rules. It was hard for the players at first ... but the results spoke for themselves.

In Guardiola's first season, Lionel led Barcelona to historic heights. The club won the Copa del Rey, the La Liga and the UEFA Champions League to secure the first treble from a Spanish team in history. There were incredible games along the way.

Lionel loved scoring twice in a thumping 6-2 victory over Real Madrid in the Santiago Bernabéu Stadium. But his favourite goal was a towering header in the Champions League final against Manchester United. It was the perfect way to wrap up a perfect season!

Lionel and the team kept on winning the next season, too. Barcelona won the Supercopa de España, the UEFA Super Cup and the FIFA Club World Cup – all by the end

 of 2009. Lionel played his part in every victory and the world took notice.

He won his first Ballon d'Or and the FIFA World Player of the Year for his 2009 season. 'I dedicate it to my family,' Lionel said after getting the Ballon d'Or. 'They were always present when I needed them and sometimes felt even stronger emotions than me.'

He was also talking about Antonela.

Lionel had lost touch with

Antonela when he moved to Spain at the age of thirteen. The two of them lived thousands of miles apart, and they had no real way of staying in touch.

But in 2005 – the same year Lionel scored his first goal for Barcelona – he flew back to his hometown and reconnected with his old friend. Lionel remembered why he'd liked Anto so much when he was younger. The pair got much closer during this time, and their friendship blossomed into something much more special.

Anto was there to celebrate with Lionel when he won that first Ballon d'Or. Lionel had told the world about their relationship, and Anto had come to live with Lionel in Spain after she graduated from university. 'The truth is that I am well and I am relaxed,' said Lionel.

That was good news for Lionel, but bad news for the rest of the footballing world. The list of things Lionel achieved in this period was phenomenal. Under Guardiola, Barcelona won three La Liga titles, two Champions League trophies, three Supercopa de España prizes, two Super Cups and two FIFA Club World Cups.

Lionel scored 211 times for Barcelona in those four seasons alone. Even his teammates started to think, *Wow! I can't believe I'm meeting Messi!*

Unsurprisingly, Lionel won four Ballon d'Ors in a row – something no one had ever done before.

'To tell you the truth this is really

quite unbelievable,' he said. 'The fourth award that I have had is just too great for words.' Lionel also made sure to thank the two most important people in his life at that time: Anto and his son.

Yes, Lionel and Anto had welcomed a baby!

Baby Thiago was born on the 2nd of November 2012. In that one moment, Lionel's entire life changed.

'He's the most important thing to me now,' Lionel said. 'He comes before everything else. Now

the way I see things has changed.
I have different priorities.'

Before, when Lionel's team lost or
he didn't play as well as he wanted,
he'd be very grumpy at home. He
wouldn't even talk to Anto about it!

'Now, when I arrive home, I see
my son and everything is OK,' he
marvelled. 'There are more important
things in life than winning or losing
a game.'

The couple had two more sons:
Mateo, born in September 2015, and
Ciro, who arrived in March 2018.
Lionel and Anto also got married in

2017 in what newspapers called the 'wedding of the century'!

Lionel was constantly amazed by his growing family, especially the kids. He'd take the boys to school before training, then watch films with them in the afternoon. The days were perfect, calm and ordinary.

This is the life I've always wanted, Lionel thought.

There was only one thing that would make his life truly complete: a trophy with the Argentina first team.

9

TOO MANY TEARS

The first time Lionel played for Argentina's first team was in a friendly against Hungary on the 17th of August 2005 ... and it was the worst debut ever!

Lionel was so excited to go on as a substitute in the 62nd minute of the game.

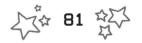

After all, he'd wanted to play for Argentina his entire life!

The ball fell to his feet almost immediately.

He dribbled towards the Hungarian goal, easing past the defender Vilmos Vanczák. Vanczák had been warned about this new Argentinian star, so he grabbed hold of Lionel's shirt to slow him down.

I want to break free! thought Lionel.

 He swung his arm back to try and break Vanczák's hold on his shirt. But his arm hit Vanczák in

the throat! Vanczák went down as if Lionel had struck him on purpose.

It was right under the referee's nose, and Lionel was shown a red card!

He'd only been on the pitch for forty seconds. Disaster!

Lionel started crying on the field, and carried on crying when he got back to the changing room. His teammates tried to comfort him, but it was no use. It was the worst thing that had ever happened to him.

It was not like I had dreamt it would be, he thought.

Unfortunately for Lionel, he'd often think the same thing after he played matches for Argentina.

For the 2010 World Cup, Argentina's coach was the legendary former player Diego Maradona – the man Lionel had been compared to his entire career. Maradona quickly took Lionel under his wing.

'I've seen the player who will inherit my place in Argentinian football and his name is Messi,' Maradona said to the public.

But Argentina and Lionel didn't perform as well as everybody wanted

during the tournament. They were eliminated in the round of 16 by Germany, and the fans were very disappointed. They'd wanted Lionel to lead the national team to glory.

Lionel said, 'I don't believe in the word "leader". I've always been the smallest on the pitch. I don't give directions. I don't talk a lot. When I have something to say, I express myself with the ball.'

But the supporters didn't even like the way he'd played.

'He didn't score a goal!' they complained.

Some Argentinian supporters started saying Lionel didn't care as much about playing for his country as he did about playing for Barcelona.

In private, Lionel cried after Argentina's defeat, and he was hurt by the criticism. But in public, he got out on the field and tried his hardest.

Nothing seemed to work.

In 2011, Argentina played in and hosted the Copa América – a competition that determines the champion of South America. The fans always have high expectations of the Argentina team, but they were knocked out in the quarter-final.

Lionel failed to find the net in any of the games, and the fans started booing him. They much preferred to watch striker Carlos Tevez.

'Messi is the best in the world,' a commentator said, 'but Tevez is the player of the people.'

Things looked like they might get better after that ... for a little while, anyway.

Lionel finally scored again for

Argentina in October 2011, and he carried on scoring for the next five years. He led Argentina to the final of the 2014 World Cup, only for them to lose to Germany in extra time.

'It's very painful to lose in the manner that we did,' he complained.

Lionel tried again at the 2015 Copa América and again got his team to the final. But the worst moment was still to come.

The final against Chile ended 0-0 and went to penalties. Lionel was the first to take a penalty kick ... and he blasted it wide!

Chile ended up winning the shoot-out and taking home the championship.

Lionel blamed himself. He broke down in tears on the pitch and wouldn't stop crying in the changing room. He cried and cried for the ten years he'd failed to win a trophy for his country.

The end has come for me and Argentina, he thought. *I wanted it so bad, but it didn't happen for me.*

Lionel told the press after the game that he'd never play for Argentina again. He was retiring from international football!

 'I think this is best for everyone, firstly for me and for a lot of people that wish this,' he said. 'The team has ended for me, a decision made. I tried many times, and I leave without being able to obtain it.'

But then something Lionel could never have predicted happened.

The Argentinian fans who'd been so quick to criticise Lionel were suddenly asking for him to stay. When Lionel landed in Buenos Aires after the tournament, supporters flocked to the airport with signs saying: *DON'T GO, LEO!*

The president of Argentina even phoned him. 'Congratulations!' he told Lionel. 'The team played a great tournament. Don't listen to the criticism!'

Maradona agreed. 'Messi must go on!'

But former teammate Dani Alves had the best advice. He said, 'These  decisions should be taken with a cold head and after a lot of thinking.'

That's exactly what Messi did. He took his time considering what he wanted to do next. He spoke to Anto, his kids and his friends. In the end, he couldn't give up the Argentina dream.

My love for my country and this shirt is too great! he thought.

'We need to fix many things in Argentinian football,' Lionel told the fans. 'But I prefer to do this from inside and not criticise from outside.'

But even Lionel's renewed passion couldn't bring Argentina

international glory. They crashed out of the 2018 World Cup, and there was more disappointment in the 2019 Copa América. The fans turned on Lionel once again.

Lionel was in pain. He wanted so badly to win a cup for Argentina, but everybody seemed to be against him. Even his son Thiago had noticed people were being mean to his father.

'Why don't they like you in Argentina, Daddy?' he asked one day.

Lionel didn't know. All he knew

was that he couldn't stop trying until he'd won a trophy!

He told his son, 'Those that don't like me will have to stand me a little longer.'

The next stop was the 2021 Copa América.

10
LIFTING THE CUP

Lionel was thirty-four when he kicked off Argentina's Copa América campaign in June 2021. He thought this could be one of his last chances to win the trophy for his country. Most footballers don't play as well as they used to after this age, so it was now or never for Lionel. But this Copa América would be especially hard for Lionel. The tournament had been scheduled to be played in Argentina and Colombia, but the COVID-19 pandemic meant all the games had to be played in Brazil without any crowds. So, while he was playing in the tournament, Lionel had to be away from his family – the most important thing in the world for him. He could talk to them on the phone, of course, but it wasn't the same.

But the pain of this separation didn't stop Lionel from helping Argentina get off to an amazing start.

They finished the group stage at the top of the table then beat Ecuador and Colombia to advance to the final. Lionel scored four goals and made five assists along the way. With each game, Lionel started to believe that this side under manager Lionel Scaloni could be the South American champions.

Only Brazil stood in their way. Brazil had won the trophy in the last Copa América, and the team had a legendary history of winning

five World Cups. They were also
playing in their own country in the
world-famous Maracanã Stadium.
If Argentina was going to win, they
needed everybody in the squad to be
at their best!

In the changing room before the
match, Lionel gathered his team. He
made them put their arms around one
another and listen to their captain.

'Forty-five days without seeing our
families, boys,' Lionel said. 'We had
an objective, and we're one small
step away from achieving it. There's
no such thing as coincidence, boys.

Do you know what? This trophy was meant to be played in Argentina and God brought it here. God brought it here so that we could lift it in the Maracanã, boys, so that it could be more beautiful for everyone. So, let's go out with confidence and calm because we're bringing this one home!'

Some of the players were in tears after the speech. They were more fired up than ever. *Let's do this!* they thought.

Argentina put their stamp on the game in the 22nd minute. Rodrigo De Paul picked out Ángel Di María, who had slipped behind the Brazilian defence. He took one touch to control the ball, and another to lift it over Brazil's goalkeeper.

Goal!

It was all the team needed to win the game 1-0!

Lionel was in a daze when the final whistle eventually blew. He knew Argentina had won the Copa América, but it somehow didn't feel real to him. After five final defeats, Lionel didn't know how to react to an Argentina win!

His teammates gathered around, kissed him, hugged him, and lifted him into the air to the delight of the few fans who'd been allowed to watch the match in the stadium.

'Messi! Messi! Messi!' the crowd chanted and clapped.

What a beautiful madness! This is unbelievable! Lionel thought. *Thank you, God! We are the champions!*

Lionel finally got his hands on the trophy, kissed it and showed it

 off to the crowd. The happiness he felt was immense.

He'd dreamt of this moment so many times, and now it was finally real.

Argentina had won a trophy for the first time in twenty-eight years!

Lionel spoke to his family as soon as he could. They sang Argentinian songs and celebrated his victory.

Lionel cried and cheered and sang and partied. He never wanted to let go of this trophy!

But in the back of his mind, Lionel knew there was still one space empty in his trophy cabinet ... and he'd only have one more shot to fill it.

WORLD CONQUEROR

'What do you want to do?' Argentina manager Lionel Scaloni asked Lionel. 'What kind of players should we have? What would work for you?'

'I want to leave everything on the pitch,' Lionel said. 'I want to carry this team to the final again. I cannot

miss that chance.'

The idea was to build the Argentina team around Lionel. Everybody wanted him to win the World Cup in 2022, and this was their best shot yet. Going into the 2022 World Cup in Qatar, the Argentinian side hadn't lost a match in thirty-six games.

We're gonna go to the World Cup, and we're going to smash every single team! the players thought.

Argentina's first match was against Saudi Arabia. Argentina was the favourite to win the game, and it looked like it was going to be a walkover when Lionel put them ahead with a penalty in the first half.

But Saudi Arabia didn't simply roll over and allow Lionel his chance to shine. They played tough and muscled their way back into the game. To everybody's surprise, they came from behind to win the match 2-1!

'This is one of the greatest World Cup shocks in history!' a commentator exclaimed.

Lionel was just as shocked as everybody else ... but he had plenty of experience with this kind of thing now. He'd lost far more important games with Argentina in the past. He knew anything could happen in football.

'Stick with us,' he told the fans and the players. 'We're better than this. We're not going to let you down.'

One thing was for certain: Argentina needed to win their final two games in the group stage. If they didn't do that, they'd be out  of the competition, and Lionel would never win a World Cup medal.

But in the next game against Mexico, Argentina didn't start well. It was as if they were still suffering from their defeat against Saudi Arabia. They were lucky to get to the half-time break at 0-0.

Lionel gathered the team around for a team talk.

'We can do this,' he told his teammates. 'We're not playing well here, but it's about winning. We can do this. We're better than them.'

After that, the players knew they couldn't let Lionel down. Many of the squad were younger than Lionel, and they looked up to him. He was their idol. They'd do absolutely anything he said!

Lionel scored a goal against Mexico in the second half, and the team eventually won 2-0. They beat Poland 2-0 in the last game, too, finishing top of the group.

Lionel stayed on the pitch after the Poland match to wave to the fans and celebrate with the team. They were a close-knit group. He felt a sense of family with them all now. It was something he'd never felt playing for his country before.

Once the matches were over, the team went back to their base at Qatar University. The team flew in 2,000 kilos of Argentinian beef so the players could host massive, traditional barbecues. They played a card game called Truco and drank maté (a traditional South American herbal drink), just like they'd have done growing up.

The younger players wondered if it would be all right just to knock on Lionel's bedroom door and say, 'Do you want to drink some maté and play Truco?'

It was all right, and Lionel had the time of his life joining in with the team. They were like a real family!

Their round of 16 match was against Australia. Lionel spoke to all his teammates before kick-off. He shook their hands to encourage them. Lionel believed in this team and knew they could win.

Lionel scored again to help his team to a 2-1 victory. He

 celebrated with his iconic pose – raising two fingers to the heavens. Every time he does this,

he's giving thanks to his grandmother who pushed him into football teams when he was only a child.

There was a party atmosphere after the Australia match, with the crowd and the players joining together to sing and celebrate. But before the next game, the tone of the World Cup changed.

Argentina would be playing against the Netherlands in the quarter-final. The two nations had met in the 1974, 1978, 1998 and 2014 World Cup, so there was a fierce historic rivalry between them. Argentina already wanted to win the tie, but then the Netherlands manager Louis van Gaal hit out at Lionel in the press.

'When they lose the ball, Messi doesn't participate much,' he said. 'That's where our chances lie.'

Lionel answered the jibe on the pitch. He assisted one goal and scored another. When Lionel celebrated his goal this time, he stood before the Netherlands bench and cupped his ears. 'I can't hear you,' that pose said.

'What were you saying? Say it again!'

But then things started to go wrong.

The Netherlands got one goal back, then levelled the game in the 11th minute of additional time. Argentina became very frustrated, and there was fighting and squabbling on the pitch. In the end, the referee gave eighteen players a yellow card and one a red card. It was crazy!

The match ended up going to penalties, and the Argentinian goalkeeper Emiliano

Martínez was the star of the show. He saved two penalties and helped his team win the shoot-out 4-3.

Lionel ran up to Martínez after the shoot-out and hugged him. 'Oh, I can't believe you've just done it again!' he said. 'You saved us again!'

Argentina breezed through their semi-final match against Croatia, winning 3-0. They had made it to the final!

Understandably, Lionel's mood was very high before the start of the World Cup final against France. The press sold the match as Lionel against the French striker Kylian Mbappé. But Lionel and Mbappé were good friends, and they hugged each other in the tunnel before the game. They were in a World Cup final, and they were going to enjoy themselves.

The match turned out to be the greatest World Cup final there'd ever been.

Argentina started the game much stronger than France. Lionel opened the scoring in the 23rd minute from the penalty spot, before Di María doubled their lead thirteen minutes later. Lionel dominated play in the middle of the park in the second half, too. France didn't even have a shot at the Argentina goal until the 71st minute!

It looked as though Argentina was going to cruise to its first World Cup victory since 1986, but Mbappé and France weren't going to go down without a fight!

Towards the end of the game, Mbappé scored two amazing goals.

 Lionel was especially gutted about the second goal because it came right after he gave the ball

away to France. He felt like he'd blown his own World Cup hopes!

Extra time came next, and it brought even more action and drama.

Twelve minutes before the final whistle, Lionel pounced on a loose ball in the France penalty area to put his side 3-2 up. Surely that was going to be the winning goal of the match.

No! Mbappé slotted home another penalty two minutes from time. He'd scored a hat-trick in a World Cup final – the first player to do that since England's Geoff Hurst in 1966!

The fans were breathless. The players were exhausted. And the game ended 3-3.

It was penalties again!

Lionel and Mbappé scored their penalties to put the teams 1-1 at the start of the shoot-out.

Then it was all down to Argentina's goalkeeper.

When Martínez saved French winger Kingsley Coman's penalty, the Argentinian crowd went wild! It was still 1-1.

Then Lionel watched with the rest of his team from the halfway line as

Paulo Dybala put Argentina 2-1 in front.

Aurélien Tchouaméni from France was next ... And he shot wide! It stayed 2-1.

Argentina's Leandro Paredes made it 3-1 to Argentina after that.

We're on the brink! thought Messi.

France put their hopes of survival on Randal Kolo Muani's shoulders. He stepped up to face Martínez ... and found the back of the net. 3-2.

Argentina only needed to score one more penalty to win the World Cup. Gonzalo Montiel was the man with

the responsibility of taking it.

Lionel stayed on the halfway line to watch. He whispered, 'Puede ser hoy, Abu.' This meant, 'It could be today, Grandma.'

Montiel took a deep breath.

The referee blew his whistle.

Montiel scored!

Argentina won the World Cup!

Lionel fell to his knees. Half of his teammates jumped on him and

 hugged him in joy. The other half rushed to congratulate Montiel.

Lionel didn't know what was happening. The day he'd always dreamt of was finally here! He'd won the World Cup!

No one could doubt it anymore: he was the greatest player of all time!

Lionel led his team to the centre of the pitch to pick up the World Cup trophy. He kissed it, rubbed the golden prize twice, then lifted it to a roar from the crowd.

'Finished! Finished!'

Fireworks exploded from the podium, and the crowd clapped and sang. Lionel couldn't get enough of it.

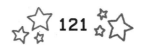

He sang and danced and cried with his teammates. He cheered and chanted with the crowd!

But the best moment was seeing his wife and kids. They were all wearing number 10 Argentina shirts with Lionel's name on the back. What a day!

It was the perfect ending to a perfect career.

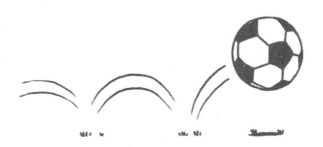

12
LEGACY

Lionel holds dozens of individual records that are unlikely to be beaten any time soon.

He scored an incredible 672 goals in 778 appearances for Barcelona, making him the club's top scorer.

He's also the top scorer in the

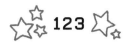

history of La Liga, thanks to his 474 goals in 520 appearances.

The ninety-one goals he scored in 2012 are the most goals any player has ever scored in a calendar year.

For Argentina, he scored 106 goals in 180 appearances – both of which are records.

Lionel has won ten La Liga championships with Barcelona, two Ligue 1 championships with Paris Saint-Germain and a Leagues Cup with Inter Miami. He's also won a record-breaking eight Ballon d'Ors.

Lionel's footballing legacy is fixed.

 His achievements speak for themselves, and players will be inspired to chase them for years to come.

But questions remain.

Can Lionel score more goals and win more Ballon d'Ors before he retires?

Will he play for Argentina in the 2026 World Cup?

When he does finally step away from the game, what will he do next?

The truth is, Lionel doesn't know. He doesn't think he'll play in the next

World Cup and doesn't think he'll be a coach ... but he's also not going to rule anything out. Only time will tell.

What Lionel is certain about is that he hopes to leave behind a legacy that's not defined by numbers and medals.

'I am more worried about being a good person than being the best football player in the world,' he said. 'When all this is over, what are you left with? When I retire, I hope I am remembered for being a decent guy.'

 Lionel has worked with UNICEF since

2010 to help do some good with his fame and fortune. He's donated millions of euros to help healthcare and sanitation facilities all over the world. He also set up the Leo Messi Foundation in 2012 to support children at risk.

'I am moved every day that I get a child to smile, when they think there is hope,' he said. 'I will continue fighting to make children happy with the same strength and dedication that I need to continue being a footballer.'

He also has his own children and family to think about. 'I want my children to do what makes them happy,' he said, and that includes playing football.

Mateo has followed in his father's footsteps, and he too doesn't like to lose! So perhaps Lionel's legacy will pass to the next Messi generation, and fans will be talking about them all for a very long time.

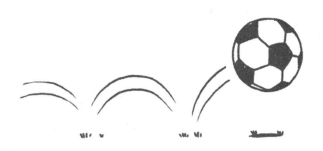